A THINGS TO MAKE AND DO BOOK
Franklin Watts
NEW YORK / LONDON / 1976

You can make and do funny things on Halloween.

You need:
- A large paper bag
- Crayons
- Scissors
- Glue
- Colored stars
- Bits of colored paper

You can make a Halloween mask.

How to do it:

1. Put the bag on your head.
2. Feel where your eyes, nose, and mouth are.
3. Mark these spots very lightly with a crayon.

Then people will not know who you are.

A witch's hat is also fun to make.

You can make a spooky bat puppet.

2. Cut out the bat.
3. Fold the bat along the lines shown.
   The center lines fold up.
   The outside lines and the head fold down.

center line

outside line

You can make a black cat.

On Halloween it is fun to color your face.

How to do it:

1. Put two teaspoons cold cream in each cup.
2. Add <u>one</u> drop of a different food coloring to each cup and mix with the stick.
3. Put the colors on your face, but stay away from your eyes.
4. A tissue and soap and water will clean you up in no time.

Halloween is also a nice time to tell jokes.

What did the papa ghost say to the baby ghost?

Fasten your sheet belt.

Many years ago there was a mean old man named Jack. When Jack died, he was too mean to go to heaven. The devil did not want Jack either. Jack had played too many tricks on him. So the devil made Jack walk all over the world carrying a lantern. The lantern was a carved turnip with hot coal inside. Now we call a pumpkin with a light inside a jack-o-lantern.

And here is a Halloween story to tell your mother and father.

Here is a game for you.

(28)

How many owls can you find in this picture?

Having a Halloween party is fun too.

(30)

Make some owls to ask your friends to come.

How to do it:

1. Draw an owl on each piece of paper.
2. Cut out each owl.
3. Color each owl any way you want.

For 24 cookies you need:

A stick of butter

¾ cup of sugar

1 egg

4 teaspoons of milk

½ teaspoon of vanilla

Orange food coloring (mix 10 drops of yellow with 10 drops of red)

1¼ cups of flour

¼ teaspoon of salt

¼ teaspoon of baking powder

Chocolate drops

1 bowl

Fork

1 cookie sheet

Bake some jack-o'-lantern cookies.

How to do it:

1. Take the butter out of the refrigerator. Put it in a bowl and let it get soft.
2. Mix the butter with the fork until it is fluffy.
3. Mix in the sugar.
4. Mix in the egg, milk, vanilla, and food coloring.
5. Mix in the flour, salt, and baking powder.
6. Stir everything with the fork until it is very smooth.

7. Put the bowl in the refrigerator for 1 hour.
8. When the hour is up, have your mother set the oven at 375°.
9. For each cookie, take 1 teaspoon of dough and roll it into a ball.
10. Put each ball on the cookie sheet and flatten it with the palm of your hand. (Don't put the balls too close together.)
11. Add the chocolate drops to make two eyes, a nose, and a mouth.
12. Bake the cookies for 8 minutes.

You need:
White bread
Cheese spread
Knife

How to do it:
1. Cut up the bread to look like stars and moons.
2. Put some cheese on each piece of bread.

Be sure to make enough for all your friends.

Make some Halloween sandwiches.

You need:

Ten pieces of white paper

Five pieces of yellow paper

Five pieces of orange paper

Crayon

Scissors

"Find the Pumpkin" is a good game to play at your party.

(38)

How to do it:

1. Draw ten white pumpkins, five yellow pumpkins, and five orange pumpkins.
2. Cut out all the pumpkins.
3. Draw a funny face on each one.
4. Write the number 1 on the backs of the white pumpkins.
5. Write the number 5 on the backs of the yellow ones.
6. Write the number 10 on the backs of the orange ones.

How to play:

1. Hide the pumpkins.
2. When your friends come, tell them to find as many pumpkins as they can before you say, "Stop!"
3. Have your friends add up the numbers on the pumpkins they found.
4. The person with the most points wins.

You need:
One small glass
Twenty kernels of corn
A chair

And you can play "The Corny Game."

How to play:

1. Put the glass on the floor.
2. Put the chair so that the back of it is facing the glass.
3. Each player takes turns kneeling on the chair and trying to drop the kernels into the glass.
4. The player who gets the most kernels in the glass wins.

You need:
- Big brown paper bag
- Pencil
- Scissors
- Record player or radio

"Get Off My Hat" is another good game.

How to do it:

1. Cut the bag so that you can open it out flat.

2. Draw a big witch's hat.
3. Cut out the hat.

How to play:

1. At the party, put the hat on the floor.

2. The players get into a straight line and shut their eyes. A leader is at the front to see that no one peeks. Whoever peeks is out of the game.

3. When the music starts, the players walk back and forth across the hat.

4. Any player on the hat, when the music stops, is out of the game.

5. The last player left, wins.

After the party, you can go with your mother or father and some of your friends and say,

"TRICK OR TREAT!"

8
Answer to
page 28

6
Answer to
page 29